"Poetry is the record of the best and happiest moments of the happiest and best minds."
– *Percy Bysshe Shelley.*

Contents

From The Manse Window

Country Calendar

The Little Water Garden

I HAVE a little garden pool, with water clear as glass,
Surrounded by sweet irises and softly waving grass.
I love to lie and listen to the tranquil, soothing tones
Of the water gently trickling, cascading over stones.

Brightly coloured damselflies flit round the grassy verges,
From underneath a rock, a tiny, timid newt emerges.
Pale water lilies float upon the surface – cream and pink,
And if I'm still and silent, birds may come to bathe or drink.

Frogs live here, too – I glimpse them crouching at the waterside.
I hear the faint, quick splashes as they swiftly dive to hide.
What other creatures dwell, I wonder, unseen and unknown –
In my entrancing pond – a little world all of its own.

– Emma Canning.

The First Warm Day

A**T** last we feel the welcome sun
As winter slips away,
And hope returns to lift our hearts
On this, the first warm day.
Green shoots are growing quickly now,
We see the earth awake,
The daffodils are dancing, too,
Beside the peaceful lake.

The birds are nesting in the trees
And butterflies appear,
The whole of life renewed once more,
Rejoice, for spring is here.
And though the showers will return
And sometimes skies look grey,
Enjoy each moment in the sun
On this, the first warm day!

– *Iris Hesselden.*

Where, Oh, Where?

WHERE, oh, where have my glasses gone?
I search, then find I've got them on!
It seems to get worse every year –
The rate at which things disappear!
And glasses aren't the only things:
There's purses, shopping, cheque books, rings.
Some are left in shops, I know,
So in and out of shops I go.
"My glasses! Did I leave them here?"
"So sorry, we've not seen them, dear."

Cheque book lost! Oh, how I shuddered –
Then found it in the airing cupboard!
My purse – now that was such a teaser,
Until I found it in the freezer!
A five-pound note (now there's a sin) –
I found it in the pedal bin!

I'm sure worldwide there couldn't be
A scatterbrain as bad as me!

– Dawn Lawrence.

Solving The Puzzle

As soon as I woke up today, I felt it from the start,
That the atmosphere was different from the usual *à la carte*.
The sun seemed so much brighter and the wind was not so keen,
As if some fairies in the night had rearranged the scene.
It could be imagination, and wishful thinking, too,
But I'm sure the sky today is a brighter shade of blue.
Could it be an illusion or was that a blackbird's trill?
And could that be, beneath the tree, a little daffodil?

Now I've just solved the puzzle of why these ideas cling,
Because, of course, we're entering another brand-new spring!

– Brian H. Gent.

Don't Look Back In Anger

I LOVE the start of a new year – it's like a gift waiting to be opened. Although I have noticed that as I get older and difficult things happen there is more of an element of trepidation these days, a sense of, "What's going to happen next?" For me, 2011 was not a good year and I had a feeling of foreboding as I approached 2012. Now, with distance, I look back and realise that we do get over things and we realise what a privilege life is and that here is an opportunity to walk with Christ into a new challenge.

I found some of my old diaries the other day. I was in my twenties, living in London with a friend and trying to make my way in the world. I remember them as exciting times as I pursued my ambitions to work in the film industry, securing a job as a secretary in a film distribution company and attending film premieres. The whole world seemed to be opening up.

Yet, reading through the diaries, I was struck by how often I commented that I felt down or unwell or really didn't want to get out of bed to go into work. In contrast to my memories, life then often seemed to be a struggle and I understand now I may have had a mild form of depression. How glad I am to be where I am now!

It's true that we can look back at the past through rose-tinted spectacles. I felt quite oppressed after reading my account of that time, but I've chosen to focus on the good times I remember and not my mood.

Sometimes people can't let go of the past or live with regrets. There's nothing we can do about the past; it happened so we can either choose to dwell on it and allow it to affect our present, or we can move on and live in the moment, looking to the future.

WHAT is important is where we are now. Yes, our lives have shaped us, but what happened in the past doesn't have to control us – every day can be a new start in Christ.

We have to be kind to ourselves. Often we hear of people who say, "I can't forgive myself", which has always seemed a bit presumptuous to me. If God has forgiven us then who are we to hold on to things and allow them to blight our lives?

A great example is Peter. He must have felt crushed after he

Thinkstockphotos.

By the Rev. Susan Sarapuk.

denied Jesus the night of his arrest. Even the joy at seeing the risen Lord again must have been tempered with guilt and a corroding sense of failure – that he was a fraud for all the big things he had said.

But Jesus takes him aside and says, "Peter, do you love me?" and then gives him a job to do: "Feed my sheep." He's telling Peter that the past is gone and that he's forgiven and now needs to look to the future and what God wants him to do.

Peter is released.

Over the years he may have gone back to that dreadful night in his mind, but then he always had the memory of Jesus's restoration of his self-esteem and his position overriding that.

We have to remember that we are on a journey, that there is more beyond this life and that in the light of eternity so much of what happens now won't matter. What matters is where we are with God and that He loves us. He promises to make all things new.

All we have is today and a glorious future which we can't quite comprehend but know is there, waiting, when everything will be redeemed. How are we living today? Are we looking back to a great past from a position of current disappointment, or feeling wounded and full of regrets because of what we did? Or perhaps we are fretting over what was done to us or the opportunities we missed so long ago? Today is what matters, and today in Christ can be a great day.

So how are we going to approach a new year? Expectations change as we get older. I'm no longer planning on flying to America to work for Steven Spielberg or winning an Oscar for writing a bestselling book which is made into a film.

In terms of church life I think my chance of being made Diocesan Missioner has gone, too. Options are more limited as we reach middle-age. We've had our careers, many of us have brought up families and there's more behind us than ahead of us, but lots of recent studies have suggested that as we get older we are also more content. Maybe that's because all those stressful life decisions are behind us and we know who we are and what we want out of life.

In Christ there is always more to come and more we can do. This is the time when we don't need to focus so much on ourselves because we've achieved what we set out to do to a certain extent.

Maybe this is the time to focus on what we can give back to church life and our communities. There was very little thought of that in my diaries from so long ago – it was all about me.

Remember what Jesus said about losing our lives in order to find them. If we put others first then our lives will be more enriched. It seems like a paradox but we prove it to be true in our experience.

The only diary I keep these days is a record of my work as a self-employed writer, but I remember the feeling of those clean pages waiting to be filled

with experiences. I want to capture again that sense of anticipation of what could happen in this new year.

We are privileged to have a new year stretching out ahead of us. So don't let your life be ruled by what happened in the past. Step out with confidence and joy. ▨

A Country Calendar For *Spring*

"April hath put a spirit of youth in everything."
(Sonnet XCVIII)

– William Shakespeare.

■ Marigolds are flowering in spring and the colourful blooms can be used in tea blends. The petals are thought to have medicinal properties and aid in easing stomach upsets and ulcers. They can taste bitter, so be sure to add some honey or sugar.

■ The first day of spring is called the vernal equinox. "Vernal" and "equinox" are Latin terms meaning "spring" and "equal night". The day is said to have 12 hours of daylight and 12 hours of darkness. This falls on March 20 this year.

Thinkstockphotos.

■ Small numbers of bees will start to buzz about at this time of year. These large, slow bees are the surviving queen bees and are searching for nectar and pollen to convert into honey for their new hatching broods.

■ The cheery daffodils are blooming, bringing with them the joy of spring and a symbol of hope. In Victorian times, they represented chivalry. In China, they represent wealth and good fortune.

FACT

"La Fête du Citron", held in February and March, is a French celebration of all things lemon. The annual celebration in the small French Riviera town of Menton is in its 82nd year. Events include extravagant parades of lemon floats, acrobats, and a lemon carnival.

■ Baby birds learn to sing during springtime. They are born with the ability to sing, but do not know the songs. They must learn the specific songs of their species and often learn them within two months of being born.

It's Got To Be Mine!

WALK past the shop, I try not to look!
I know it's still there, still hung on a hook.
I feel my heart thump – I want to go back.
I'm finding it hard – willpower I lack.

I'm starting to sweat; it's now hard to breathe.
I know I'm a mess, I really should leave.
I see it right now, it's simply divine.
It's got to be mine, it's got to be mine!

I have to go back, it's waiting for me.
I have to go back – it's just got to be!
Temptation is bad, it's going to win.
I have to go back, it's pulling me in.

I'm inside the shop, I hold my purse tight.
She's taking it down, I must look a sight.
She brings it to me, and asks me to sit –
She is putting it on, I hope it will fit.

I look at myself, I'm starting to smile.
I've wanted it now for such a long while
It's there on my head – I watch myself preen.
The hat is now mine! I feel like a queen!

– Sandra Stoner Mitchell.

21

The First Picnic

SUN poured through the window and beckoned to me,
From dull, dreary weather I longed to be free.
The cold days were passing more quickly, it seemed,
The day looked inviting as everything gleamed.

So filled with bright sunshine, refreshed by soft rain,
The scene held such promise of warm days again.
Excitement now rising, I jumped out of bed,
As outings and picnics were filling my head.

Persuading my loved one to go for a ride –
We laughed as we packed. Soon the car was outside.
A tonic it was when long weeks had been grey,
We blossomed, found joy in this promising day.

Our lunch in the car kept cool sea breezes out.
We watched seagulls preening and strutting about.
Refreshed as we walked, we absorbed everything,
For we had enjoyed our first picnic of spring!

– Chrissy Greenslade.

My Dream Garden

MY cottage garden's truly grand –
It's beautifully arrayed.
I gaze around it as I stand
And lean upon my spade.

Perfumed roses climb the wall,
Near towering hollyhocks,
And at my feet, a riotous sprawl
Of daisies, pinks and phlox.

Nasturtiums, lupins, dahlias,
A radiant peony,
Chrysanthemums, azaleas –
All glorious to see.

Yes, here I'll spend some carefree hours –
Sit quietly enchanted.
But – oh, dear me! – right now, these flowers
Sit waiting to be planted!

For they bloom only in my dreams –
My garden's not yet growing.
I've lots of work to do, it seems –
I really must get going!

– Emma Canning.

Spotted

WE spotted a great spotted woodpecker
Tapping a hole in a tree.
With its head forward bent,
It drummed with intent,
Seeking insects to take for its tea.

It was maybe the size of a starling,
And handsome, black-chequered with white,
But its tail flashed with red
When it passed overhead.
It appeared very bright when in flight.

Very soon it was joined by its partner –
They made such a sweet matching pair.
Was their nest in the tree?
With some fledglings, maybe?
We'll keep watching in case it is there.

– Dorothy Morris.

Renewal

As spring comes dancing through the woods
With palette in her hand,
She dips her brush and splashes colour
Right across the land.
It seems that all the countryside
Is clothed in misted green,
As swelling buds and tiny leaves
Appear upon the scene.

From feathered throats come fluted notes
Floating on the breeze,
And catkins dangle dainty tassels
Trembling on the trees.
The daffodils are shooting through
With heads up to the sun,
Crocus cups and bluebells, too –
And primrose time has come.

There is a freshness in the air –
Renewed vitality,
For all of nature's bursting forth
With strength and energy.
For spring has brought a sudden surge
Pulsating through the earth,
Awakening all the dormant things
And bringing them to birth.

– Kathleen Gillum.

Sun Success

EACH day was chilly and each day more rain –
Everyone longed for warm weather again.
Then smiles returned, what a lovely surprise,
As the sun won its battle with dark sullen skies.

Cobalt the sky and azure-painted sea,
Waves splashing, fish dashing and gulls flying free,
Powder-puff clouds changing shape and their shade,
As brave gorse, aglow, faces winds unafraid.

As the sun's resting behind hazy cloud,
With today's triumph it now can be proud,
Its strength and its grit has brushed our blues away,
And given us a beautiful, bright, cheerful day.

– Chrissy Greenslade.

30

A Baker's Dozen

WE have a baker in the town
Whose bread is of the best.
I went to buy some little rolls,
Then said to him, in jest:

"I think I'll have a dozen."
He put twelve aside for me.
I didn't like to argue –
I'd no wish to disagree.

Yet many years ago at school
How well we all were taught,
A baker's dozen is thirteen,
Cheaper if more are bought.

And there were sundry adages,
"Too many cooks" was one,
Another said that "Many hands"
Made work a bit more fun!

Oh! How I loved these proverbs
That the old wives used to say,
Sagely nodding of their heads
To point me the right way.

Are they all forgotten
Those sayings that I knew?
A few were contradictory,
But many more were true!

— *Dorothy Morris.*

New Beginnings

AS the year rolls on, we see new green shoots appearing in the ground and leaves reappearing on the trees. But actually these buds and flowers have been there all along, and water and warmth were the only things necessary to show what was already there. They had been lying dormant all the time, perhaps even as invisible seeds under the ground, until we probably believed there was nothing there.

Then they suddenly spring up, proving that spring has come at last and those plants and trees were alive all along. They were not dead after all!

Jesus's last words from the cross, "It is finished", were not marking the end. It would be better to describe them as a "completion" – and there is a difference.

His mission on earth had been completed and soon there would be the emotional moment of his ascension into heaven. A wonderful thing had been accomplished and now there was a chance to let something new begin.

The signs of new life are all around us at this time of year, as baby animals make their appearance in the world. Little lambs and baby chicks produce "oohs" and "aahs", but we await their appearance as a sign that the seasons are changing.

WHEN my children had to move to a new school, I told them how lucky they were to be given a chance to go over some old ground and perhaps, I argued, redoing a subject they were familiar with would iron out any misunderstandings and also give them a superior advantage over their classmates if they knew all the answers.

They weren't fooled! They were both more concerned about those subjects that would be new to them – they were bothered that they would appear ignorant for not knowing anything about a subject they had never been taught before.

You see, spring comes around every year – but next week's maths test doesn't!

A "new beginning" can be a challenge – but they were more concerned, as all schoolchildren are, that with spring comes school holidays!

I think they found the anticipation of the new school

Thinkstockphotos.

By Kathrine Davey, Methodist preacher.

▶ was probably harder than being there. Like my children in their new school, God was doing something completely new.

As we look forward to Easter, I am reminded that God puts us in a completely new landscape – and it takes time to adjust and to get our bearings. Like my children, no matter how much we want to, we cannot go back to our old school.

A new page in an exercise book gives us a challenge to write more neatly, to work harder or to be more successful, but the extraordinary soon becomes ordinary. The same is true of starting anything new – whether it is a new workplace, or moving to a new area. Yet, despite our nervous anticipation, we soon get to know our new colleagues and neighbours.

I think it creates a great problem that the run-up to Easter has become so familiar. Perhaps because Good Friday – and even Easter Sunday itself – are often treated like normal working days.

We hear references to the "bank-holiday weekend", and many people do not know why it is there at all. Like the clean page, it soon loses its thrill, or its relevance to learning.

M Y memory of school holidays was that they seemed to stretch out way into the future. They seemed never-ending, yet only too soon we were making all sorts of preparations for returning to school.

Often nowadays the school holidays seem to serve no real purpose in a lot of people's minds, other than to give them a bit of chocolate and a few weeks' break from work or from school.

Perhaps the holidays are a chance to do a bit of DIY or some other job around the house. They leave us with a lot of time on our hands and so we waste it, by doing something – anything in fact – just to fill it up. Unfortunately, to many people now, Easter means nothing. When the Easter season ends, they return to "normal" life.

How many of you can remember getting your first television or some modern labour-saving device? Yet the younger generation seems so casual and accepting of new technology and quick to adapt to new devices – putting the older generation to shame. The great life-changing experience that particular object brought to our everyday lives is no longer thought about by most of us at all.

However, the thought of the great change that Easter brings to our Christian faith cannot be underestimated. A musical person might consider this new life in terms of a new key. In fact, the keys or the strings of the instrument were there all along, but it takes a musician to reveal the life in them. Many Christian martyrs and people who have changed the course of history have done so because of what Christ did at Easter.

If the first witnesses to Jesus's Resurrection had returned to the tomb again, they would still have found it empty, so they had no option but to live life in light of the Resurrection. They could have stayed where they were, but that would have served no purpose. They had to keep moving on, to

proclaim "He is risen", to obey the angel's words to "go and tell".

And they did – and the church was born.

The approaching Easter holidays are usually at a bit of a crossroads in the seasons, when we are leaving behind those long, dark days of winter and getting ready for the warmer summer days. But, never forget, people down the ages have changed the world because of what happened during those very first Easter holidays. ■

A Country Calendar For Spring

"Our spring has come at last with the soft laughter of April suns and shadow of April showers."

– Byron Caldwell Smith.

■ The beautiful azaleas are coming into bloom this time of year. Although their name comes from the Greek word for "dry", this only refers to the Lapland variety of azaleas that will only grow in dry places and does not refer to the modern varieties.

■ Padstow in Cornwall holds its annual Obby-Oss (Hobby Horse) day of festivities on May 1. Revellers dance with the Oss through the streets, accompanied by accordion players and followers dressed in white with red or blue sashes who sing the traditional "May Day" song.

■ A Greek Easter tradition is the game *tsougrisma* (knocking together). Eggs are boiled and dyed red to symbolise the blood of Christ. The aim of the game is to break the other player's egg by tapping it with your own, but not breaking your own egg in the process.

■ Radishes are a fast-growing crop and grow from seed to eating plant in 25 days. This makes them the first UK field-grown salad vegetables to come into season in April. Over 8,000 tonnes of radishes are sold each year in the UK alone.

FACT

"I Wandered Lonely As A Cloud" by William Wordsworth was inspired by a "long belt" of daffodils on a walk he took on April 15, 1802. The poem was first published in 1807. Though not well received in his lifetime, it is now one of the nation's favourite poems.

■ Although rabbits build nests, they do not stay on or by the nests after the babies are born. This attracts the attention of predators. Instead, the babies burrow to the bottom of the nest where they remain hidden until the mother rabbit wakes them up at mealtime.

A Springtime Prayer

DEAR Lord of all the seasons,
We thank you for the spring,
We thank you for the hopefulness,
The promise it can bring.
We waited for the spring's return
Through winter dark and drear,
We longed to see the daffodils
And knew they would appear.

Now through the sun and shadows,
Through rainy days or bright,
We'll listen for the blackbird's song
And reach out to the light.
Dear Lord of all the seasons,
Be with us every week,
And let the springtime fill our lives
With all the joy we seek.

– Iris Hesselden.

41

At Last!

AT last here comes the sunshine!
At last the sky is blue!
It's rained and rained for always!
(All right – it's nearly true.)
I'm leaving off my raincoat,
My brolly's staying furled,
I'm cheerful as a sunbeam
To see this fine new world.
And yet – I must admit it –
If always days dawned bright,
I'd miss out on this feeling
Of sheer amazed delight!

– Maggie Ingall.

Can You Guess?

NOW what is bright and prickly
And makes us think of spring?
It's golden yellow, cheerful,
And brightens everything.

It's seen on moors, in forests,
On cliffs, beside the sea.
On hillsides, dales and roadsides,
It flowers abundantly.

A glorious mass, a background,
For rabbits, deer and horse,
You've guessed by now, I'm certain,
You're right, of course, it's gorse!

– Chrissy Greenslade.

Sweet Wonderment

W**E'RE** going on a Maytime treat
Along the country lanes
To see the lovely blossom there,
Dewed by the spring's light rains.
Small golden yellow kingcups,
Purple lilac on the breeze,
The lady-smocks in dainty pink –
May chooses all of these.
Our thankful spirit soars on high
On magic Maytime wings,
And dreams of all the wondrous gifts
This glorious season brings.

– Dorothy McGregor.

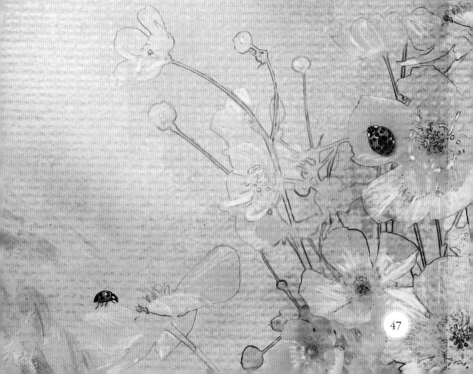

Healing Green

PALE green and dark green, moss green and lime,
So many summer shades,
In cottage gardens, hills and dales
And all the leafy glades.
The gentle green of summer days
In sunlight or in rain
Can touch the heart and calm the mind
In street or country lane.

The city dwellers cherish plants
In window-box or pot,
And now and then escape to toil
In some suburban plot.
Dame Nature gives year-round delight
With every changing scene,
But nothing soothes the human soul
So much as healing green.

– *Iris Hesselden.*

Going Away

OUR holiday's coming, just three weeks to go,
I've bought clothes that I'd normally hate,
Plus shorts for the kids and T-shirts for John
And I'm counting the days – I can't wait!

Now it's only three days to our going away –
There are lists coming out of my ears.
If I don't sort the packing for both of the children
I know it will all end in tears.

So our holiday time is finally here,
You should see the stuff piled in the hall –
When I think of the washing, the packing, the travelling,
It's hardly worth going at all!

– Eliza Barret.

Books

WHATEVER my mood or the time of the year
I know that I can depend
On trusty old books that have served me well –
Each one such a well-loved friend.

In winter you'll find me tucked up in my bed,
The morning still dark outside,
The glow of my lamp and my tea within reach,
My cat snoozing at my side!

The garden's the place on a summer's day,
Curled up in a shady nook,
The scent of the flowers, the hum of bees –
My nose in another book!

I wish I could thank all these authors of old
Who bring me such joy every day.
Without them my life would be poorer by far –
A debt I can never repay.

– *Eileen Hay.*

The Village Wedding

WE traipsed up the cobbles, avoiding nettles
(And petulant flowergirls hurling petals!)
The warm sun shone down on our happy faces –
All of us decked out in satin and laces!

The old church was tranquil with sunbeams beaming
With jewel-bright light from the windows gleaming.
The bridegroom was standing so pale and quaking
And we all plainly saw that his poor knees were shaking!

The organ then started, the sound so uplifting
And in came the bride with her veil gently drifting.
We all wiped a tear at her youth and her beauty.
The best man was solemn, aware of his duty!

And then it was over, their new life beginning,
The bridegroom, relaxed now, just couldn't stop grinning!
Out into the sunshine the air filled with laughter
I wished them both happiness for ever after!

– Eileen Hay.

from the Manse Window

What A Difference A Day Makes!

VERY often, whether preaching from a pulpit, speaking in public or writing for books and magazines, it has been my practice to introduce my thoughts in the title or words of a song.

Do you remember the erstwhile lyrics, "What a difference a day makes, twenty-four little hours"? It was originally written in Spanish by a Mexican songwriter but was later translated into English by Stanley Adams, and it is most associated with the singer Dinah Washington.

My purpose in quoting the song here goes back much further than the 1950s. Indeed, I want to go back to the dawn of the first century, to the day when the world first celebrated the glorious Resurrection of Jesus Christ from the dead, and I want, ultimately, to exclaim, "What a difference a day makes!"

However, before we identify and quantify the unspeakable difference that day must surely have made, we should transpose the song title into question form, namely, "Did the day (Easter Day) make any difference?"

There are some aspects of this world-shattering event, at least in the early days after the first Easter, which demand our attention. If we ask what difference the first Easter made to many closest to Jesus, we immediately discover that, really, it didn't make any obvious difference to them or to the world of the day.

Pilate was still Governor of Judea after Easter as he was before, Caiaphas was still the High Priest, the Scribes and Pharisees still dictated and directed religious life. The road to Jericho was still a risky road on which to travel, the tax collectors still bled the ordinary people dry at every opportunity, the money changers were still operating there in the Temple porch and Rome still ruled supreme with an iron rod.

And the ordinary people, if they realised at all what had happened outside the Jerusalem city wall on Good Friday and in the Garden of Gethsemane on Easter morning, soon forgot about it. In no time at all they were back to business as usual.

HAVING said all that, we must go on to say that the first Easter Day did make a tremendous difference in the lives of a few people, because it made them realise that what had looked like failure was not failure.

By the Rev. Ian W.F. Hamilton.

▶ Instead of thinking that all Jesus had stood for – things like forgiveness, trust, confidence and love – had been denied on Good Friday, they slowly came to see in a kind of strange yet victorious kind of way that all Jesus had died for had been affirmed.

The spirit of Jesus and of his way of living had somehow got inside them and they began to live for the kind of things he lived for. They were ready for anything, and to take on anyone. In this frame of mind, they went out from behind their locked doors in Jerusalem in the strength of all that Jesus had died for, absolutely convinced that nothing could ever separate them from the love of God in Jesus Christ their risen Lord!

What we are really saying is that, realistically speaking, the Resurrection of Jesus – at the time – didn't suddenly reform the world. Rather it raised up a few people who were willing to live the Christian way of life despite anything the world might mete out to them.

The difference the day made – at the time – didn't immediately transform the world, albeit inwardly it made a powerful difference in the lives of a few faithful followers.

Again, looking realistically at things, has this not been the pattern down through the ages and generations, looking at Easter from a world-wide perspective? Easter Day comes, and it goes, making, on the face of things, no great apparent difference, yet inwardly it has made a powerful difference, because each year Easter Day continues to make a tremendous difference in the lives of men and women.

WHEN I was studying Divinity at the University of Glasgow and Trinity College many years ago, I was privileged to have as one of my lecturers the Rev. Professor Murdo Ewen Macdonald. Murdo had served as a chaplain in the Army during World War II. He was dropped behind enemy lines, wounded and captured.

He spoke of an incident when he was serving as chaplain to American prisoners of war. He told of how he had learned about the invasion of Normandy and of D-Day, when early one morning an American soldier shook him awake shouting, "The Scotsman in the British camp wants to see you, and it's terribly important!" Running to the barbed-wire fence separating the British and American camps, Macdonald met up with MacNeil, who had been in touch with the BBC by underground radio. MacNeil spoke a couple of words in their native Gaelic, "They have come!"

Murdo Ewen Macdonald then flew back to the American camp as fast as his legs could carry him and began arousing the soldiers.

"They have come, they have come!"

Again and again he said it. The reaction was incredible! The men jumped in the air, they ran outside, they hugged each other, they shouted at the tops of their voices and they rolled on the ground with ecstatic joy!

Their German guards thought they had gone crazy! After all, they were still prisoners of war, nothing had outwardly changed, but inwardly they knew it

was different. They knew that things were going to be very different. Freedom was on its way and life was about to begin again for them anew!

On the face of things – at that time – no apparent difference was evident, but that day in 1944 helped change the course of history . . . that's the difference that day made!

In a comparable kind of way, slowly, quietly, subtly but steadily and surely, the Church of these early disciples, which, remember, was only the beginning, has grown and grown. In the world today, it is still growing by thousands and by millions year in, year out.

Although things in the world post-Easter may look much the same as they did pre-Easter year after year, we mustn't be deceived! The difference Easter Day made, and will continue to make, must never be understated, because that day makes all the difference in the world! ▥

A Country Calendar For *Summer*

■ Father's Day, the holiday designed to partner Mother's Day, was supposedly founded in Spokane, Washington in 1910 by Sonora Smart Dodd. Her father was a war veteran who had raised six children on his own. It wasn't until the latter part of the century that it caught on.

■ School summer holidays around the world are traditionally based on the idea that the children would be free to work in the fields and help out with farming. Several countries are challenging the relevance of this these days, including the US, where some schools operate on a two months on/one month off programme.

"If the first of July it be rainy weather, 'Twill rain more or less for four weeks together."

■ With recent years being so cold, hawthorns are frequently only blooming in June now. Hawthorns have been harnessed by humans and animals to provide shelter or protection, their fearsome thorns proving almost impenetrable. Despite the fact we generally see them as hedgerow plants, trimmed and shaped for our protective or divisive use, when they're left alone they can grow into strong trees as tall as 14 metres, approximately 15 yards!

Thinkstockphotos.

There are about 900 donkeys still working on UK beaches. Weston-super-Mare's famous donkeys have been working since 1886 and the business is still run by the same family. Dark-coloured donkeys are preferred for beach work, as they are less prone to sunburn.

FACT

July was the fifth month in the early calendar of the ancient Romans. The Romans called the month Quintilius, which means fifth. A Roman Senate renamed the month to Julius (July) in honour of Julius Caesar, who was born on the 12th day of the fifth month.

The name strawberry comes from the Old English words *streowberie* or *streawbelige*. There are two theories as to why they have this name. The "straw" bit could come from the straw that was put around to keep the strawberries fresh, or from "strew", which means to spread wide.

Don't Forget
To Dream

OH, I remember childhood dreams –
Exciting plans and reckless schemes
I'd cherish, and in secret keep –
Back then, when dreams weren't just for sleep.

How easy, now, to leave neglected
Hopes we nurtured and protected,
And, when grown, become resigned
To leaving childhood dreams behind.

Yet now could be the time to start
Rekindling dreams within your heart.
Life's many opportunities
Are moments that are there to seize!

For dreaming should be so instilled
That as each fades, or if fulfilled,
Another swiftly takes its place –
So, always, there's a dream to chase.

New skills, adventure or ambition,
Longed-for goals brought to fruition,
Or just making time to spend
Some precious moments with a friend.

For all dreams, whether old or new,
With perseverance, may come true.
Keep looking forward, eyes agleam –
And don't ever forget to dream!

– Emma Canning.

63

The County Show

BEN CLARK was a hard-working farmer,
And he loved family life, without doubt,
And Ann Clark had only one grievance –
It was seldom he took them all out.

Ben was not eager to travel,
He muttered, he hummed and he hawed,
Then he said they could go
To the next County Show
If Ann promised they wouldn't get bored.

On the great day they dressed up like gentry –
Ann had a new dress and a hat,
Then she tried to get Ben to wear his best suit
But he put his foot down on that.

So Ben took his chance to see tractors,
For his machine needed a part,
And he met with two men
He'd last seen, now, when?
It must have been last cattle mart.

Ben's whole day was spent in the same tractor tent,
For they were dispensing free beer.
When the time came to go, home from the show
Ann had to drive, that was clear.

Said Ann, "That was grand" as she patted Ben's hand,
"We've had such a fine day – lovely weather.
It's made me feel good, just as I knew it would.
There is nothing like being together."

– Dorothy Morris.

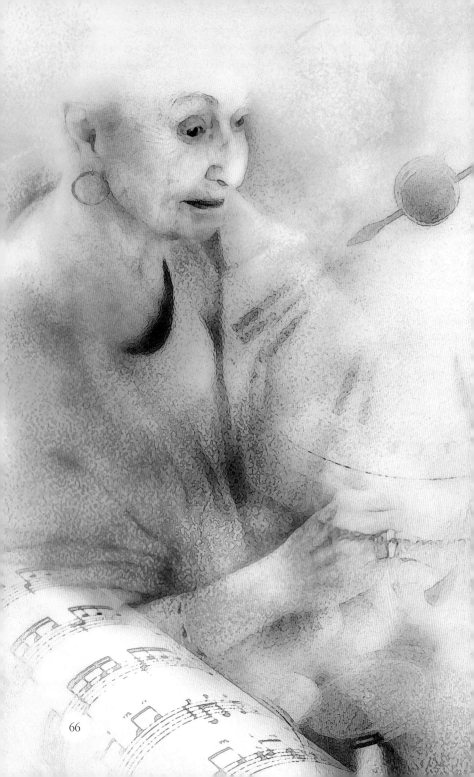

Things I Miss!

THE feminine feel of a silly high heel –
(It was always the highest I'd choose!)
But these days, my friends, I ignore all the trends
And just head for the comfiest shoes!

I loved pretty frills which would peep out in spills
When I did a quick twirl on the floor!
We'd dance half the night and wake up breezy bright! –
We all thought we'd be young evermore!

Without any fuss I would run for a bus,
Never knowing a puff or a wheeze!
I'd dash up the stairs in my life without cares
And with never a twinge in my knees!

How much one forgets, but I have no regrets,
I take life at a much slower pace!
My life is content and my days are well spent.
It's good just to walk and not race!

– Eileen Hay.

Perfect Day

REJOICE to the sun at morning,
Healing in warmth and light,
Starting the day with gladness,
Making the world so bright.
Look to the golden morning,
Bringing a cheerful mood,
Setting aside a moment,
Feeling your hopes renewed.
This is a time when summer,
Presenting a perfect day,
Shows us God's lasting blessings,
Protecting along our way.

– Elizabeth Gozney.

Shells

WHO would think a fragile shell,
Could have the powers to retell
Those magic times of pounding sea,
That ran in foam-filled filigree,
That, when held close to the ear,
Brings memories back of sounds so dear.
Those endless days, so blue the sky,
The wheeling, diving seagull's cry,
Buckets, spades and miles of sand,
In a unique fairyland,
Such are the wondrous special spells,
Held in the folds of simple shells.

— *Brian H. Gent.*

Beautiful Roses

OUR days delight in the magic array
In joy of the fragrant rose,
Twining around the summer's heart
And spell of enchantment flows.
Dewed by the rain this lovely flower,
So favoured and fair of face,
Hues of yellow, pink and red
And white our paths will grace.
In a garden of heavenly flowers
An exquisite bouquet, we see,
These beautiful summer roses
So beloved by you and by me.

– Dorothy McGregor.

The Hummingbird Hawkmoth

HOVERING by the lavender
I was surprised to see
A creature like a hummingbird,
As strange as it could be.

Its head was dark and smoky,
Its tail was flecked with white,
Its tiny wings, fast beating,
Shone golden in the light.

Some diurnal hawkmoths
Disguise themselves as bees
As they feed upon the flowers
And flit amongst the trees.

All are welcome in my garden,
But isn't it absurd
To see a little hawkmoth
That thinks it is a bird!

– Dorothy Morris.

The Kindness Of A Stranger

WHAT Paul wrote about the peril of money explicitly emphasised that it is really the love of money that is "the root of all kinds of evil". For money, in its proper function, lubricates commerce as the vehicle for all trade and barter.

It is certainly a basic measure of Christian living as expressed in the Acts of the Apostles when Luke says "It is more blessed to give than to receive" and yet again when Matthew says "Freely you have received" – presumably from God – "so freely give!"

How much more our gratitude when we receive money wholly unexpectedly when we need it urgently, as indeed was my own experience one particular day in May 70 years ago.

It was VE Day, the end of the long, dark days of the war, and celebrations were very much in order. We had lived through over six years of blackout with darkened streets as protection against enemy bombers. The wardens came round to check on the slightest display of light from a semi-closed curtain and they were not slow to impose fines upon us if they found any.

Years later, when I had the opportunity to travel in a plane, I realised how needless those precautions were, since it proved nigh impossible to see even a shop window display from above!

I was living in Glasgow at that time and when I heard that Edinburgh Castle was to be floodlit for the first time since 1939 as part of the victory celebrations, I decided I had to be there. Even though I had often visited Edinburgh, I had never seen the castle floodlit.

My father had fairly recently rewarded my exam successes by giving me a bike, and though, until this point, my use of my new bike had been local and the distances modest, I could see no problem about cycling 50 miles to see my favourite castle floodlit.

MY plans were quite simple. I would cycle to Edinburgh, see the floodlit castle, then cycle on to Birkenside where my aunt Kate lived. Aunt Kate was always pleased to see me, even when I turned up with a couple of my Scouts. She would look after us all for two or even three days at a time. ▶

Thinkstockphotos.

By Arthur J. Brown BD.

So, setting off in the late afternoon of VE Day, I arrived in Bathgate about seven o'clock and went to the local chip shop for a fish supper. It was only then that I realised with dismay that I had left my wallet at home lying on the dressing table. However, searching through my pockets, I was relieved to find I still had just enough money as long as I spent it carefully.

I eventually reached Edinburgh by early evening and sat on a bench close to the Scott Monument in Princes Street Gardens watching the world go by, and glancing up occasionally at the floodlit castle looking like some fairy palace floating in the clouds!

The immaculate maroon and cream Edinburgh tramcars trundled along with festival flags streaming on their trolley ropes, and every so often I turned to gaze up at the floodlit castle, and I felt it more than worth all the effort. Finally, about 10 o'clock, I set out for Birkenside, which was a further 15 or 20 miles on, and Aunt Kate.

As I pedalled up the hill, the rain started to fall gently, but I encouraged myself with the thought that I would soon be snug and dry in Aunt Kate's house. But as I turned the corner where she lived I had an ominous sinking feeling on seeing that her house was in darkness. She had gone on holiday!

There was nothing else for it but to turn homeward and make my way back to Glasgow through the rain, which by now had become a downpour getting heavier by the minute.

Reaching Edinburgh, I was too tired to go any further and so I decided to shelter for the night in Waverley Station, intending to continue my journey first thing in the morning. I lay down on a station bench to snatch some sleep when out of the corner of my eye I saw a policeman approaching me. He proved to be quite friendly, asking where I was heading. I told him I was heading to Glasgow.

ABOUT six in the morning I got ready and pushed my bike across the concourse to begin my journey back to Glasgow. The rain was still falling.

The same kindly policeman urged me to take my bike by train. I took no persuading, but when I went up to the booking office window and asked the price of a ticket for myself and one for my bike, I was told that the cost of both tickets would be 27 shillings and sixpence. I realised immediately that I was far short of anything like that money. It may not seem much all these years on, but it was more than I had for my weekly wage on the farm where I worked.

But even as I stood there wondering what to do, the kindly policeman reached over my shoulder and placed a pound note and three half crowns on the window ledge. I picked up the two tickets and turned to thank my benefactor, but he had vanished, unthanked, quickly into the crowd.

And so, as I sat in the warmth of my homeward-bound train, watching the rain lashing against the carriage windows, I felt filled with a surge of warm gratitude to the kind policeman who had made my return journey possible. And even now, 70 years on, I still feel a surge of gratitude when I think about

his kindness.

"But who IS my neighbour?" people asked of Jesus. And Jesus replied with the parable of "The Good Samaritan".

Certainly, from my own experiences, the world is full of such Good Samaritans, and we can thank God for the occasions on which we find them. Or perhaps, more often, that they find us!

It is with sustained gratitude that I still remember the Good Samaritan in a policeman's uniform who helped me on that particular morning. ■

A Country Calendar For Summer

■ Sometimes it seems there's a themed day for every day of the year! In fact, there almost is, with June seeing the celebration of Sewing Machine Day, Go Fishing Day, World Milk Day and Armed Forces Day, amongst others.

■ Head to Wales this month for the annual Eisteddfod, a giant celebration of Welsh culture. With origins going back as far as 1176, the festival is held alternately in north and south Wales, to give everyone who lives there a chance to make it along.

"Oh, the summer night, has a smile of light, and she sits on a sapphire throne."

– Barry Cornwall.

■ This is harvest time, and the country is alive with fruits and vegetables at their very best, including home-grown tomatoes. But did you know that throughout the 1600s Brits avoided eating them as they were certain they were poisonous?

Thinkstockphotos.

August 12 is known as "the glorious 12th", as it marks the start of the grouse season.

Estates up and down the country open their land to shooters in hope of a prize, although for many it's as much about enjoying the great outdoors and time with friends.

FACT

It's National Catfish Month in America in August, when the country celebrates one of its favourite farmed fishes. The biggest wild catfish caught in the States weighed 59 kg (130 lbs) – as much as a small person – but this pales in comparison to the giant Mekong catfishes of the Far East. The largest of these caught on record weighed an almighty 293 kg (646 lbs)!

The flower of the month for August is the gladiolus, which symbolises remembrance, sincerity and strength of character. They take their name from Roman gladiators, as their stalks resemble swords.

Lazy Afternoon

ALONG the river,
Very fast,
A motor yacht
Is speeding past.
A pleasure boat
Comes chugging by
And children wave
To passers-by.
Here and there
Are small canoes
And rowing boats
That gently cruise,
Avoiding ducks and geese
That float
Oblivious of the motor-boat.
The banks are high
With meadow-grass,
And old men
Watch the traffic pass.

– Dorothy Morris.

Sunrise

SPECTACULAR and beautiful
Is sunrise of the day,
The sky is splashed with cream and gold
As colours interplay,
From peach to flame and pink to mauve
Then red with orange hints,
The clouds awash with morning light
Are flushed with rosy tints.

As sunrise steals upon the world
The birds wake up and sing,
A sudden stirring on the earth –
A skylark's on the wing.
And everything is bathed in light
With coming of the sun,
And all of nature springs to life –
A new day has begun.

And as I gaze upon the scene
Set out before my eyes,
It seems an artist's canvas has
Been spread across the skies.
The splendour and magnificence
Quite takes my breath away,
I'm lost in awesome wonder at
The sunrise of the day.

– Kathleen Gillum.

Summer

DOWN among the buttercups,
Where the dry seeds blow,
Grasses and wild flowers
Happily grow.
Bees come to visit,
Butterflies swarm,
Swift fluttering pheasants
Sound the alarm.
Blackbirds are singing,
Fledglings appear,
There is warmth in the sunshine,
Summer is here!

– Dorothy Morris.

Swallows

On a day that is almost September,
Torn between sun and wind,
Like ice skaters curling the sky
They loop and skirt and lift –
Little miracles made of air.

They nest in the eaves of our porch;
Sometimes at night I open the door to the dark
To catch their jostle in the tiny light.

All these weeks and we don't even know
Their number. The young ones find the sky
As easy as breathing; catch and swivel
In a dance the same since the beginning.

Then, as though some voice has summoned them,
The swallows gather:
Africa restless deep inside,
Thousands of miles in their wings.

The following day they're gone, all of them –
And we watch where they were, wondering.

– Kenneth Steven.

The Bottomless Drawer

R UMMAGING through my kitchen drawer –
Surely these aren't all mine?
A tape rule, corkscrew, battery,
A tangled ball of twine.
What's this strangely shaped utensil?
I wonder what it's for?
Blue candles for a birthday cake –
My serendipity drawer.
A Scrabble tile, a bent nail file,
My grandson's bouncy ball;
Matches, screws and elastic bands,
How did I collect them all?
One solitary wooden chopstick!
Will I ever find its pair?
And the item I was searching for?
Sadly, it wasn't there!

– Patsy Harris.

A Glance Away

DESPITE the dullness of the day,
And rain cascading down,
I only need to glance away
To stop a sigh or frown.

Such colours soon bring on a smile,
A warm content; a glow.
My TLC was so worthwhile
To bring forth such a show.

Should rain and mist persist for hours,
This cannot dull my pleasure.
The beauty in my vase of flowers
Is something that I treasure!

– Joan Zambelli.

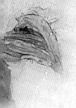

Ruby

SHE is a very tidy cat, she doesn't shed much hair.
She wipes her feet upon the mat, and doesn't scratch the chair.
Black lines surround her topaz eyes, like kohl, and amber fur
Adorns her belly, soft as down. There's comfort in her purr.

Her paddy paws are snowy-white above, and pink beneath,
And when she yawns, so daintily, she shows her lethal teeth.
She has a tiny appetite, for very little mice,
And when she was much younger she brought frogs in, once or twice.

She has her favourite place to sit, at the corner of the stair,
And often bends unblinking gaze on something that's not there.
Curled like a cashew nut, she lies beneath me as I write,
One paw across her eyes to hide her feline dreams from sight.

My Ruby, pretty kitty cat, I treasure more than gold.
We'll keep each other company, as together we grow old.

– Sue Weait.

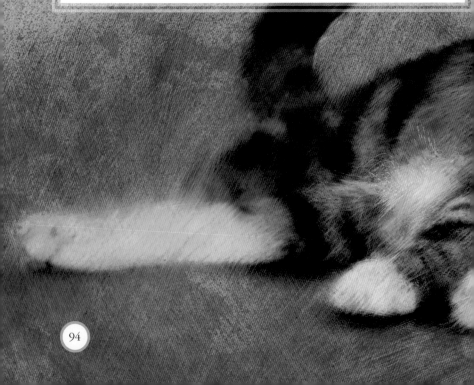

The Magic Of Autumn

TAKE a walk in the magic of autumn,
  Through nature's flamboyant display:
Sudden colour pervades –
Vivid, luminous shades –
And the summer slips softly away.

The bright coral pink of the spindle,
The claret of maple and gum;
Witch hazel and ash
Lend a pure yellow splash
To the splendour the woods have become.

The musky, rich, earthy aroma
Enhances this glorious show.
And the mellow sun pours
On to damp forest floors
Prompting circles of fungi to grow.

Oaks yield a profusion of acorns –
Provisions for jays and for squirrels;
Every sycamore key
Tumbles down from its tree
To be caught on the wind as it twirls.

And branches bear fruit in abundance –
Just right for a sweet autumn tart.
With a handful of cherries,
Or ripe hedgerow berries,
You'll bring autumn home to your heart.

– Emma Canning.

from the Manse Window

Rest And Renewal

I EXPECT most of us are planning to take a holiday some time during the coming year, but what we choose to do will vary. Some people like to be active and explore while others just want to relax; some like to go abroad while others prefer to stay at home; some like camping, others like luxury hotels.

Whatever our choice, it's all about taking time out for refreshment and recharging the batteries.

Everybody needs a break from work or routine. People who are carers may need those they look after to go into respite care so that they can have a break from the responsibility. Those being cared for may benefit from a change of scene and company, too.

After a summer holiday there's a sense of getting ready for the new challenges as autumn is just around the corner. Perhaps that feeling is tied up with the beginning of the academic year which all of us have experienced since childhood. Some people say it's often better to start a diet or fitness campaign in September rather than in January.

So to have a wind down before everything kicks off again is a good idea. For many of us it might be the only time we have a proper break as life has become so hectic. The concept of a day of rest every week is enshrined in the book of Genesis right at the very beginning of the Bible, when God rested on the seventh day after creation. In today's society, however, with 24-hour shopping, mobile phones and the internet, we seem to have lost that idea, even though it's essential for our wellbeing.

We just keep going until we run ourselves into the ground and then we wonder why we're so irritable and not able to get things done efficiently.

Even Jesus's disciples had to take time off. The demands around them were overwhelming, the need obvious and constant, yet Jesus took them aside so that they could rest.

SOMETIMES going away seems like too much effort; the choosing of the destination, the booking, making arrangements for pets to be looked after, worries about leaving our home. Then there's the stress of actually travelling, particularly if you have to use an airport. But the benefits are worth it. Most people when they ▶

Thinkstockphotos.

| By the Rev. Susan Sarapuk. |

▶ return are glad they made the effort.

Often going away gives us a different perspective on life back home. It enlarges our world and helps us to see things we couldn't see when we were in the middle of them. It can help us to be kinder, too, because we're more relaxed.

So going away renews and refreshes us, but having a holiday also gives us the blessing of memories to bring out and savour over and over again.

When I was growing up, my family never went on holiday. The only one I can remember is when I went to university and that summer, for the first time ever, my parents, my brother and I went to Butlins for a week of particularly blustery wet weather.

As soon as I was earning I started taking an annual holiday, mostly coach tours which are a great thing if you're travelling alone and also if you want to see a lot of things in a short space of time. So I've been to both the east and west coasts of the USA, the east coast of Canada, France, Italy, Switzerland and Austria.

I have piles of photos and daily diaries I can pull out periodically and reminisce over. Having those memories is much more important to me than having expensive things in my home. It was money well spent because I came home with new experiences of the world and a feeling of being ready to face life and all its responsibilities with new vigour.

Now family commitments mean I wouldn't be happy to leave for any length of time so I prefer not to go away. I have to admit that I miss it.

In the meantime, escaping for the day is still a break. One day to do something different, visit a new place and see new things is something most of us can manage.

WHEN Jesus took his disciples aside for a break it wasn't a whole week. Maybe it wasn't a whole day, but they had to have time to themselves, away from the clamour of the crowds and the needs around them.

We shouldn't feel guilty about taking our break either. I know a lot of clergy who won't take a day off, but they are not indispensable and they have to take care of their own needs, too.

On one occasion Jesus went out early to pray. His disciples came looking for him. "Everybody in the town is looking for you," they said.

The previous day Jesus had taught and healed and obviously the hunger for more was still there; people still had needs to be met. They, and the disciples, expected that Jesus would return and carry on where he'd left off the day before. Instead he said he had to go on to the next place so that he could preach the gospel.

"You will always have the poor with you," Jesus said on another occasion, pointing out that they could never expect to meet all the needs of humanity.

Nor can we, even though we sometimes feel we ought to.

It is good to step aside and find rest and renewal. Then we come back to our responsibilities feeling reinvigorated with a host of good memories to

sustain us. After heat, sunshine and relaxation we can look forward to the cooler days of autumn and everything starting up again as we head towards the frenzy of Christmas. ▧

A Country Calendar For *Autumn*

> "No spring nor summer's beauty hath such grace As I have seen in one Autumnal face"
>
> – **John Donne.**

■ Figs are in season now, but did you know that fig trees don't blossom externally because the flower is on the inside of the fruit? Many tiny flowers inside the fig create the seeds that give it its texture!

■ September 15 has traditionally been Japan's annual Respect for the Aged Day, although after 2003 the day was moved to the third Monday of September. This is due to the passing of the "Happy Monday System", new laws which dictated that some public holidays should be moved to Monday to allow workers a three-day weekend.

Thinkstockphotos.

■ In this month, back in 1825, the world's first public railway service began between Stockton and Darlington in England. Truly the start of an era!

In spite of its name, the real Bavarian Oktoberfest actually starts in mid-September, running through to the first weekend in October. It was originally set up as a festival to celebrate a Royal wedding in 1810, and the year after it was supplemented by an agricultural show that still runs to this day – although obviously these days it's most famous for its association with beer. Only beer that's produced within the city of Munich may be drunk at the festival.

FACT

Although there are plenty of memorable quotes about September, you won't find any in Shakespeare – he never mentions the month once in all of his works.

Share the benefit of your best perennials by collecting the seeds from them before the weather turns. Just a few minutes of work gives a lovely present for friends or family.

Finders Keepers

I **FOUND** a purse the other day, which someone else had dropped.
I could have kept it for myself – instead, I thought and stopped.
A lucky find for me, perhaps, but was it mine to keep?
For wiser ones than I have said that what you sow, you reap.
By taking time to give things back, no matter what the cost,
You find you keep some precious things, which otherwise are lost.
It means you keep your conscience clear; you keep your peace of
  mind.
Your honesty, your self-respect, you also keep, you'll find.
These things will prove more valuable than all the gold around,
For those who think of others will the happier be found.

– Rachel Cherrington.

Harvest Time

EACH year I love it
When September comes,
When the trees in the orchard
Are heavy with plums,
When apples are bending
Their branches down low,
And out in the hedgerow
Are brambles and sloe.
Our big wicker baskets
Are filled to the top
With richness and ripeness
Not found in a shop.
And the cupboards are filled up
With jellies and jam
And lovely fruit chutney
To eat with the ham.
And I'm glad of God's bounty
And thankful that I'm
Gathering the fruit
At each harvest time.

— *Dorothy Morris.*

The Country Fair

THE country fair, in days of old,
We greeted with delight.
The entertainments, booths and stalls
Were such a splendid sight.

The range of goods that folk could buy
Was colourful and wide,
And there were sports and contests, too,
And even more beside.

For children there were toys and games,
And cakes and sweets as well,
And hours and hours of fair-time fun
To hold them in its spell.

Although it came but once a year,
It brought folk so much joy,
And lots of happy memories,
For every girl and boy.

– Rosemary Bennett.

Walks On Cooler Days

IT'S lovely to go walking out
On cooler autumn days,
When there's a hint of morning mist
Which turns to golden haze.
A time when trees are shedding leaves
Their colours bold and bright,
And spider webs hold gems of dew
All sparkling in the light.

A nimble squirrel buries nuts –
He hardly makes a sound,
As conkers with their chestnut sheen
Come plopping to the ground.
When fruited boughs are laden down
And trees are all ablaze,
I do enjoy just taking walks
On crisp and cooler days.

– Kathleen Gillum.

Gift Of Heaven

A NEW baby's an aspect of heaven –
It's a drop of perfection, a pearl.
It arrives on this earth pure and simple
Disguised as a boy or a girl.

It's a tiny new life, it's a promise,
Brand-new hope for future unknown.
Its unique little form and its beauty
Is there to be shared till it's grown.

God has sent this pure, sweet individual
To bring light to our lives with its charm.
It's a chance to enjoy and to cherish
This gift and protect it from harm.

So before it is touched by the earth plane,
While it's innocent, faultless and true,
Let us cloak it in love and devotion,
So God's child will receive what is due.

– *Chrissy Greenslade.*

Autumn Glory

THE sky is blue, the clouds are high,
Yet teasing winds go sneaking by,
Some red-brown leaves are here and there
And we feel autumn in the air.
The summer came and went too soon,
With rain in May and storms in June,
But now we sense there's something new –
Another season here in view.

A time for peace and autumn dreams,
To put aside all useless schemes,
To smell the wood-smoke on the air
And see more colours everywhere.
And though there's mist along the fell,
Let autumn weave its magic spell.
Now let the wonder play its part
As autumn glory lifts your heart.

– Iris Hesselden.

Childhood Memories

LIKE to remember when I was a child –
Such different times from today –
We skipped with our ropes and bounced balls on the wall,
Hopscotch in the playground we'd play.

We'd make up our games – we imagined them all –
No computers, mobiles or TV.
In the outdoors we played, free as air, unafraid,
Then bread, jam and cake for our tea.

How happy we were as we played in the field
Making camps with the sun-dried cut grass,
And, oh, what excitement when the circus came!
How we longed for our school day to pass.

We would race out of school to the massive Big Top,
Laugh at clowns, gasp at flying trapeze.
Then in summer sometimes we'd catch fish in jam-jars,
And play hide and seek behind trees.

How excited I was as the summertime came
To be wearing my crisp cotton frock,
In my white ankle socks – oh, what joy we had then!
How I wish I could turn back the clock!

– *Chrissy Greenslade.*

Gather The Harvest In

AUTUMN, the "season of mists and mellow fruitfulness", is the time for gathering in crops. Over the years I have come to realise what a great blessing the harvest is. During the war, when I was a young child, food was in short supply and the order of the day was ration books. I was brought up not to leave anything on my plate and to say a silent grace before eating. Nothing was wasted in those long-gone days. Even bones were boiled to make broth.

We kept chickens and any eggs not immediately needed were placed in large iron buckets containing isinglass, a thick, glue-like substance that prevented them from going addled. The alternative was powdered egg, which was not very palatable.

Our garden had a large variety of fruit trees growing and there were several shelves in one of the outhouses that were used for storing apples. Some varieties kept for months, although by Christmas they became somewhat wizened with shrivelled skin and dry flesh. We still ate them because we were hungry.

Another way of saving for a rainy day was to bottle fruit in Kilner jars.

This was a task that my mother took seriously. The fruit-filled bottles were placed in a large tub and boiled for several hours. Glass lids with a rubber washer underneath were screwed on.

After the jars had cooled they were lifted up by their lids. If the tops came off, the vacuum had failed and the whole process had to be done all over again. The larder was filled with bottled rhubarb, pears, plums, raspberries, blackberries, gooseberries, blackcurrants and even cut-up quinces. The fruit padded out many a thin wartime meal.

ON a high shelf in the vicarage kitchen, well away from the blackleaded range, was a towering pile of 14 lb tins of corned beef that my father had bought for emergencies. Corned beef hash was served up frequently and we ate it gratefully. To this day, I can see those tins with *Buenos Aires* written on them, for they came from Argentina. The empty shelves in the grocer's shop and our grumbling stomachs brought home to me the importance of the harvest. It was something for which to be profoundly thankful.

The years went by and I was ▶

By the Rev. David Bryant.

ordained into the church and went to work under the watchful eye of an experienced vicar. There was considerable poverty in the 1950s and in the past a local had left enough money to provide a sack of coal for every old person in winter. My task was to organise the distribution of the sacks and I invariably ended up well sprinkled with dust and grime and suffering backache from heaving the sacks into cottages.

The Harvest Festival service was always a big occasion and we sang the hymn heartily:

"Come ye thankful people come,
Raise the song of harvest home;
All is safely gathered in,
Ere the winter storms begin."

The fruit and vegetables and flowers decorating the church were all put to good use. I was given a list of some 40 or 50 needy parishioners who would appreciate a harvest gift and I was responsible for dividing up the produce. It wasn't easy because marrows and swedes were unpopular and everybody wanted bananas, oranges and apples.

It was always good to see the delighted faces of the recipients, although I remember an elderly lady complaining that she hadn't got any grapes. Fortunately I was able to conjure up some from a pile of fruit that had been missed because it was behind the font!

IN my late forties I realised that the harvest is not confined to Great Britain. It happens all over the world. We were touring through some of the remote parts of Tunisia one day and we drove past a stretch of desert and saw the local school in action.

A group of some 20 children were sitting down in the sand, writing on slates overlooked by a female teacher dressed in black. They were under the shade of some palm trees and beside the children was a string of haughty-looking camels.

I was looking at part of the local harvest, for camel milk and cheese are staple foods for desert dwellers because the animals can survive the harsh conditions.

We drove on down to the Sahara desert and stopped at a village miles from anywhere. Most of the houses had been hollowed out underground and had rooms connected by winding passages. We soon realised why – even in early June, the thermometer was reading 100 deg. F. in the shade and it was the only way of keeping cool.

A friendly family beckoned and insisted on showing us their beautifully neat underground home. I still remember the lovely pieces of needlework hanging up on the walls.

One woman was cooking a large pan of couscous or steamed semolina, and it suddenly came to me that I was looking at another part of the North African harvest. What amused us most was when a party of Tuareg or nomadic desert men came into the village to buy food. Despite the intense heat they were

120

muffled in thick woollen jackets, scarves and heavy trousers. For them, it was a cool spring day!

We reached an oasis and encountered a different harvest altogether. High above our heads in the branches of palm trees hung great clouds of dates. There were stalls set up under the trees where men and women were selling them. We bought a bagful and they were delicious. Nothing like the variety you can sometimes buy in this country.

I had always thought of the harvest as being apples, pears, plums, potatoes, cauliflowers and the like. But this visit to Tunisia reminded me that the world is filled with an amazing variety of fruit, vegetables, pulses, nuts and foodstuffs, many of which are unknown to us.

The Jesuit priest Gerard Manley Hopkins wrote a poem called "Hurrahing In Harvest." Perhaps we should take a leaf from his book and do just that. For the harvest is truly one of the earth's most blessed gifts. ▦

A Country Calendar For Autumn

Thinkstockphotos.

"Listen! The wind is rising, and the air is wild with leaves, We have had our summer evenings, now for October eves!"

– Humbert Wolfe.

■ It's time to dig up the carrots! But did you know they are one of the very few vegetables that are actually marginally more nutritious cooked than raw? The cooking process simply makes it easier for us to digest the goodness.

■ Did you know that when the leaves change colour, they are actually returning to their natural colour? The chlorophyll that makes them green is only present during the growing seasons of spring and summer. As the leaves reach the end of their annual life, the chlorophyll withdraws and allows the other pigmentation to show through.

■ Although we all tend to put away our cameras after the summer holidays, winter reveals a whole other side of nature that's worth capturing. Keep an eye out for the year's first frosts – the glistening cobwebs are very photogenic.

The Hallowe'en tradition of witches carrying broomsticks possibly dates back to elderly, poor women who lived in forests and were often the source of folklore about the existence of witches. Without horses, they would use sticks – or brooms – to give them support as they walked through the forest.

FACT

The changing of the clocks was the brainwave of a British man called William Willet. Thinking that Londoners wasted too much of summertime in bed, and because he resented his summer golf rounds getting cut short by the light, he furiously promoted his suggestion to Parliament until his death in 1915. The next year, in 1916, the idea was adopted when it was thought to help the war effort.

October is traditionally the start of English pudding season. Although we use "pudding" today to refer to sweet dishes, it was originally used to refer to anything stuffed and cooked in a skin or even a cloth – like haggis, black pudding or clootie dumpling.

The Harvest
Of Spirit

THE harvest is gathered, the crops are brought in,
Give thanks, now, for fruit and for grain,
The bounty of nature, gifts in good measure
All blessed by the sun and the rain.
The harvest is needed to feed everyone,
The help every day to begin,
But fruits of the spirit sustain us
And nourish us daily within.

The harvest of spirit is faith, joy and peace,
With hope for tomorrow today,
With beauty around and love in abundance
And guidance to show us the way.
Rejoice in the harvest and all the earth gives,
Give thanks for the blessing you find,
Reach out to each other with trust and with love,
Share the harvest with all of mankind!

– Iris Hesselden.

Purls Of Wisdom!

I'M pretty proficient at knitting –
I've jumpers galore to my name.
I make tops and elegant dresses,
And no two are ever the same.

I knit and I purl and I cable –
I'll run up a shawl in a trice.
And so I was truly delighted
When my granddaughter asked for advice.

"Please, Gran, would you help with a pattern?
Could you show me the way to cast on?"
Of course, I declared that I'd love to.
Well, it's high time my skills were passed on!

"What will you be making?" I asked her.
"A hat, or some warm woollen clothes?
Perhaps a tea cosy or handbag?"
Yet she shook her head – none of those.

So, what is our new knitting project?
I suppose I should really have known.
It's not woolly toys, scarves and blankets –
But a case for her mobile phone.

– Emma Canning.

Portrait Of Seasonal Grace

MICHAELMAS DAISY of autumn
Glowing in colour today,
Vibrant and rich as the season,
To welcome and brighten our way;
You're part of the floral arrangement
That nature prepared through the year,
Presenting an intricate pattern
Of beautiful blooms to appear.
Summer's display is now over;
Autumn now takes pride of place,
Bringing fresh views to enchant us –
A portrait of seasonal grace.

– Elizabeth Gozney.

If Only . . .

IF only I could see again
   through a baby's eyes,
When everything was new and fresh
   and full of sweet surprise,
Like looking at a flower
   and a flitting butterfly,
Or at those far-off fluffy things,
   floating in the sky.
Dozing in my brand-new pram,
   cat-net in its place,
Coverlet to keep me warm
   edged in crocheted lace,
Or to have an hour's kip
   in my straw-clad cot,
To wake up to roast beef and veg
   served from a little pot.

But, alas, my fantasies are
   simply reverie,
For tomorrow is my birthday
   and I'll be seventy-three!

– Brian H. Gent.

The Coming Of Winter

WINTER is approaching –
Icy weather lies ahead.
It's time to pack light shoes away
And bring out boots instead.

And out, too, come the heavy clothes:
My favourite woollen sweater,
And trusty knitted cardigans –
For warmth, there's nothing better!

Hot chocolate and a cosy fire –
Well, what more could I need?
It's chilly out – a good excuse
To snuggle up and read.

And as the frost forms on the glass,
My thoughts are warming, too:
I'm dreaming of hot crumble and
A steaming bowl of stew.

Outside, on winter evergreens
Bright berries will appear.
They'll bring to mind a joyful thought –
Soon Christmas will be here.

And so I'll welcome wintertime
Despite the cold and wet,
For I love the changing seasons –
Winter? Oh, yes – I'm all set!

– Emma Canning.

A Prayer

THE winter seems a long time, Lord:
A long time until spring,
A long time till we see green shoots
And hear the small birds sing.
So whilst the days are short and dark
Please keep us safe and strong,
Let cheerful music lift our souls,
Place in our hearts a song.

Through wintry winds, through frost and fog,
Let every doubt dispel,
And let your love fill all our lives
And whisper, "All is well."
We thank you, Lord, for home and food,
The blessings of each day,
Let hope and joy light up our world
Till winter slips away.

– *Iris Hesselden.*

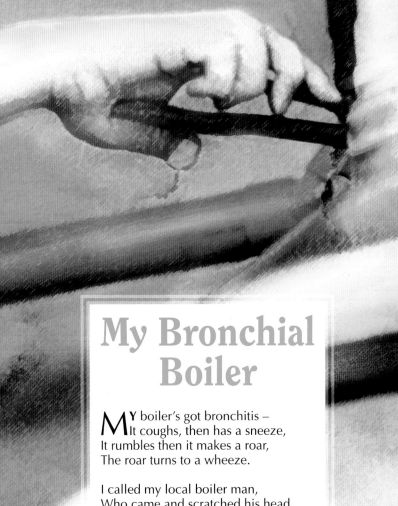

My Bronchial Boiler

MY boiler's got bronchitis –
It coughs, then has a sneeze,
It rumbles then it makes a roar,
The roar turns to a wheeze.

I called my local boiler man,
Who came and scratched his head.
"It could be one of many things –
Or something else instead.
Its pump might well be faulty,
It could be this – or that."
His words did much to cheer me –
I thanked him much for that.

He said, "Just wait till winter's gone,
The wheeze is bound to ease,
But now just hope it doesn't stop –
For if it does, you'll freeze!"

– Dawn Lawrence.

Serenity

THE glorious rays of setting sun
   Show up in etched relief
The stillness of the tawny owl;
A sighting – all too brief!
Then drifting by horizon's rim,
Thus fades the final ray,
And darkness makes its swift descent
To blot all trace of day.

The tawny owl is stirring now
And silently swoops by,
Intent upon nocturnal haunts
With sudden, hooting cry!
The myriad stars on velvet black,
Though distant orbs of light,
Now add enchantment to the scene,
And beauty to the night.

– Elizabeth Gozney.

Songs For The Season

COOLER days are here and every evening we seem to put the lights on a little earlier and leave the heat on a little longer! With the prospect of the darker, colder months, people adjust to a different programme. The lawnmower and barbecue are stored away in the shed and we start thinking more of indoor activities. For many, the simplest option is to curl up in their favourite chair with a cuppa and watch TV. Others enjoy a quiet read, or the crossword.

The autumn and winter months tend to be busy in churches, with our loyal volunteers busy running a programme of activities for all ages. Men's meetings, women's meetings, uniformed organisations – there's hardly an evening when there's not something going on in the hall!

When I get a night in the house I'm not a huge TV fan. I prefer to relax by playing guitar, trying to remember old tunes and perhaps attempting to figure out some new ones.

I'm told that years ago, in the days before all the piped entertainment and multimedia gadgets we have now, people used to go "rambling" and gather in friends' homes for a bit of company and a chat. Maybe someone would sing a song, or if someone had a musical instrument they would strike up a tune and others could join in. Hence was born folk music. Sounds right up my street!

Music is a universal language which transcends borders and communicates on many levels. Occasionally while travelling on the Continent I've been drawn into impromptu jam sessions with strangers of various nationalities and language has never been a barrier – we've just let the music do the talking!

MUSIC is such a powerful vehicle for human expression in a host of different ways.

Take, for example, the intimidating beat of the drums of war. Or the soothing strings of an orchestra playing a lullaby or backing a romantic song. What about the exuberant, up-tempo swing of a dance band?

It seems we have a music style suited to just about every emotion we humans experience. ▶

Thinkstockphotos.

By Rev. Andrew Watson.

▶ That variety is reflected in the Bible's "hymn book", the Psalms. We may be most familiar with them in the metrical form as they appear in the Psalter, which was being used in Scottish kirks from the 17th century.

Many of us have enjoyed singing Psalm 23, "The Lord's My Shepherd", to the tune "Crimond" or Psalm 95, "O Come And Let Us To The Lord", to the tune "Irish" – with or without an organ!

Of course, these days many Psalms have been rewritten in new forms and may be accompanied in some churches by a praise band. A blend of traditional and innovative can be tasteful and inspiring and, most importantly, honouring to God as the one whom we worship! I always insist that the instruments and tunes are not nearly as important as the content of the words and the humble, heartfelt attitude of our hearts.

L EAFING through Psalms in the Bible we discover 150 varied songs for very different occasions. While a number of the writers are named and some of the songs are anonymous, most are attributed to King David who, even as a shepherd boy, seemed to have considerable talent as a musician and song writer. I wonder how he would have fared on "Britain's Got Talent"?

Scripture does tell us that when King Saul got into one of his foul depressions, David's melodious playing on the harp would bring relief to the troubled monarch.

Some Psalms are designed for personal devotion, praise or prayer:

"To You, O Lord, I lift up my soul; in You I trust, O my God." (Psalm 25 v 1)

Or this famous one which actually speaks prophetically of Christ a thousand years before He was born:

"The Lord's my shepherd, I shall not be in want." (Psalm 23 v 1)

Some are more liturgical, written to be used in gatherings for public worship:

"Shout for joy to the Lord, all the earth.

Worship the Lord with gladness;

Come before Him with joyful songs."(Psalm 100 v 1 – 2)

Some are painfully honest cries of lament, the Old Testament equivalent of "blues" music:

"How long, O Lord? Will You forget me for ever?

How long will You hide Your face from me?" (Psalm 13 v 1)

Some are deeply penitential, like this one after the prophet Nathan confronted David about his adultery with Bathsheba and murder of her husband:

"Have mercy on me O God . . .

Wash away all my iniquity and cleanse me from my sin . . .

Do not cast me from Your presence or take Your Holy Spirit from me."

(Psalm 51 v 1, 2 and 11)

The one uniting theme through them all is the writers' faith in God, often tried and tested, but always shining through in the end:

"God is our refuge and strength,
An ever-present help in trouble.
Therefore we will not fear,
Though the earth give way
And the mountains fall into the heart of the sea . . .
The Lord Almighty is with us;
The God of Jacob is our fortress." (Psalm 46 v 1 – 3 and 11)

John Calvin called the Psalms a "mirror" for the human soul, for here we find reflections of all our moods and experiences – happiness and sorrow, confidence and doubt, exhilaration and depression, victory and defeat. Their inclusion in the Bible encourages us to believe that ordinary, flawed human beings like us may actually approach Almighty God and be heard.

We should come with the praise and thanksgiving and reverence of which he is worthy. But also with simple honesty, expressing our feelings to our loving heavenly Father who knows and understands and welcomes our hearts' cry, who listens to the music of our soul in every season of life. ▨

A Country Calendar For *Winter*

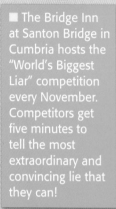

■ The Bridge Inn at Santon Bridge in Cumbria hosts the "World's Biggest Liar" competition every November. Competitors get five minutes to tell the most extraordinary and convincing lie that they can!

■ As the continental Christmas markets spring up around the place, many of us will doubtless enjoy a glass or two of mulled wine. Lightly spiced wine is one of the most common winter traditions there is, with countries including Japan, Brazil, Russia and Canada having their own versions.

"November comes and November goes, With the last red berries and the first white snows."

– Elizabeth Coatsworth.

■ Writers unite every November in the event known as NaNoWriMo – National Novel Writing Month! To participate, you have to pledge to write 50,000 words by November 30. It's both an attempt to focus the efforts of all of us who have ever thought about writing but never quite got around to it, and to do so as a community – sharing the experience with the hundreds of other doing it!

■ Enjoy a taste of Christmases past by roasting the season's first chestnuts. Easy and nutritious – they are the perfect fast food!

■ November is often the first month when we feel winter's bite, with temperatures dropping nationwide. But spare a thought for the citizens of Yakutsk, a city in north-eastern Russia, where November means an average temperature of -27 deg. C., with a record low of -54.5 deg. C. With an average of only 60 hours of sunshine for the month, you'd need a strong constitution to live there!

FACT

The famous author, poet and gardener, Vita Sackville-West, once said that November was amongst the favourite months of the year for gardeners, as it's an opportunity to tidy up, clear the beds and devote time to planning next year's efforts.

■ All around the country, winter sees brave swimmers taking to open water for various events. Christmas Day dips, New Year dooks, Boxing Day baths – you name it, people are doing it! If you've ever thought of giving it a go, the general consensus is that it's best to lower yourself in slowly to get used to it, rather than jumping straight in . . .

Jumping In Puddles

I SAW a child jumping in puddles
With giggles and squeals of delight,
In blue wellies, green jacket, red brolly,
With smiles and eyes shiny and bright.

I had muttered before setting off for the shops
That the storm clouds were heavy with rain
And I'd had quite enough of the weather,
It was so cold and rainy again.

But watching him I was reminded that
Each storm cloud has something to give,
That we have to embrace every moment,
Go splash in those puddles and live!

– Eliza Barret.

Summer Memories

THE gentle lapping sound of waves
And salty tang of spray,
The sunshine sparkling on sea foam
And children at their play.
Rockpools, seashells, sailing ships
Picnics on the beach,
Tossing bread to crying gulls
Swooping within reach.
These sunny summer memories
I will recall once more,
When winter in his icy robes
Comes tapping at my door.

– Kathleen Gillum.

My New Electric Mixer

THE electrical mixer I purchased
Was a gadget I felt I would need,
And upon a first careful inspection
I found it had more than one speed.
I selected the speed least aggressive,
(Once I'd stirred the ingredients in),
And then a great whirring and grinding ensued,
And, oh! What a mess I got in!

The cake mix prepared with such effort
Erupted and shot in my hair!
The windows were full of brown splodges;
The currants were glued everywhere!
The cat, who was watching with interest,
Received a great blob on her nose!
And I was encased in a "mummy-like" shroud
That covered me down to my toes!
I now had a new kind of wall paint
Adorning my kitchen like glue;
A kitchen décor that was somehow unique,
Resembling a kind of beef stew!

So my mixer now has a label,
A warning that reads, *Red Alert*
When using this, please take precautions –
And wear your old trousers and shirt!
I'm suspicious now of all new gadgets
That supposedly save one some pain.
I think I'll go back to the old way
Of using a fork once again!

– *Dawn Lawrence.*

Dentist Ditty

I TRY to read a magazine,
Intending to distract
My mind from pain and fillings,
And the thought he might extract.
A patient's hand is trembling,
Some pretend that they are brave,
Their faces giving them away,
Twitching, nervous, grave.

The distant sound of drilling
Fills each heart with fear and dread,
The thought of those now present is,
They wish they'd stayed in bed.
I practise yoga methods
To keep calm and act my age,
Glad mine is just a check-up,
As I turn to the last page.

– Chrissy Greenslade.

Embers Of The Day

THE burning cinder of the sun
  Descends with rosy glow
Upon the red horizon's rim,
Suspended deep and low.
A giant orb of crimson fire,
Like some eternal eye,
Casts out its rays of radiant flame
Across the evening sky.
And as the sun sinks in the west
And disappears from sight,
The dying embers of the day
Merge softly with the night.

– *Kathleen Gillum.*

Contentment

ON Sunday evenings by the fire
I think of many things,
I close the curtains on the world
And soon my thoughts have wings.
I think of other winter days
And walking in the snow,
Of snowball fights and Christmas lights
And those I used to know.

On Sunday evenings, peace returns
To soothe my heart and mind,
I let the troubled world go by,
Last week is left behind.
Though people hate the wind and rain
And winter makes them tire,
I find contentment in my heart
On Sunday by the fire.

– Iris Hesselden.

Time To Rest

AFTER summer's busy harvest,
After autumn's windy rush,
Comes the quietness of winter,
With its peacefulness and hush.
Nature seems to take a breath,
Settles down to sleep and rest,
Saving energy for springtime,
To awake with joy and zest.

Did you know that there's a lesson
Which in wintertime is taught?
Time for rest and slumber,
Be it long or be it short,
Will refresh our tired spirits,
Make us lift our heads and sing,
And we'll start again empowered,
With the gloriousness of spring.

– Rachel Cherrington.

A Child Is Born

AT this time of year when the days are getting colder, our thoughts often turn to a time that will cheer us up and take the edge off the dreary days of winter – that is, Christmas, and the preparations for it which almost seem to last all year. However, before Christmas Day is here and gone, there are lots of other events which are almost as much a part of Christmas as the days itself.

One of the most memorable and tear-jerking occasions is often the school nativity play, where the proud parents and grandparents take lots of photos and videos which will embarrass their children in the future!

Every year brings small boys as shepherds rushing round with tea towels on their heads and wise men with their boxes wrapped in gold-coloured paper and empty perfume bottles, which they lay before a manger holding a plastic doll. The innkeeper is often well-rehearsed in shaking his head and saying no.

Last year, I was at a play where the whole audience was surprised when the small child concerned was encouraged to utter the word "yes", although he quickly added, "but only if you can afford it," and Mary and Joseph couldn't.

I have witnessed nativity plays which stretch the imagination somewhat to incorporate a vast cast of everyone in the school – including mice in the stable and the innkeeper's very large family. The play usually ends as those watching become emotional when they witness a version of "Away In A Manger" sung with great enthusiasm by all the children present.

THE school or Sunday school teachers are often presented with a difficult choice in deciding who will take the principal roles in this annual dramatic performance. After all, it is not just the children, but also all their relatives, that will be affected.

However, the Biblical account makes it plain that many of the participants in the events that first Christmas had little choice in their roles in the story. Mary and Joseph were obliged by Roman law to go to Bethlehem, the home town of Joseph's ancestors.

If they had been able to make a decision about it, I am sure they ▶

Thinkstockphotos.

By Kathrine Davey, Methodist preacher.

would have preferred not to travel that far, because they knew that by that time Mary would be heavily pregnant, and they could tell by the crowds setting out that it would prove very difficult for them to find somewhere to stay.

Mary was presented with a choice by the Angel Gabriel on whether to participate and, fortunately, she did. Joseph was also presented with a choice of whether or not to continue his relationship with Mary, knowing that it would attract the scandal of the village.

The innkeeper's choice was tempered with sympathy for this mother-to-be and her (undoubtedly) harassed husband. However, he was a businessman and had no choice but to show them to his smelly animal shelter.

So, Mary did not even have a proper bed for her newborn baby. There was no midwife to attend the birth and it must have been frightening for the teenage girl to give birth in such strange surroundings. It was even stranger to think that this was the Son of God, coming down to earth in such a primitive way. I am convinced that this was a way of showing that God identified with the homeless and socially deprived of our society.

This was affirmed in God's choice of the group of shepherds that were the audience to the angels' announcement that the Saviour had come to earth. They were not the little children that we are so familiar with from the school nativity play, but tough working men who did an unpleasant job which meant being away from their families for a long time.

They had a choice as well – whether to stay or whether to go. They decided to go, and showed they had chosen wisely by becoming the first witnesses of this miraculous baby lying in a manger.

THE other witnesses could not have been more different. The only mention of the three wise men is in the Gospel of St Matthew. Unlike the picture so beloved of Christmas cards, they were not present at the stable, but Scripture tells us that they came to the house where the child was, so it was likely they arrived some time after.

Nowhere does it say there were only three of them – but as they presented three gifts, this was the version that was adopted. They had probably begun their journey long before Jesus's birth and like many of the others involved with the Christmas story, they, too, had a choice, as they had to decide whether to undertake this hazardous journey or not.

They were possibly Zoroastrian astrologers from Persia, not the kings of Christmas carols. Upon seeing a star rising in the east (the Star of Bethlehem), they realised it was a sign that the King of the Jews had been born, and so their journey began.

As they presented their "Christmas shopping" to the infant Jesus, they worshipped him, showing that highly educated, wealthy men at the other end of the social scale were included, too, in Jesus's mission.

The 12 days of Christmas show that the celebrating of this special Christian feast used to go on to January 6, which is often referred to as the Epiphany.

This is a special day in the Christian year, when we commemorate the visit of the three kings, or wise men, to the young child (no longer a baby).

This touching tableau so familiar to all of us is proof then that everyone, of any background or age, is included in celebrating Jesus's birth. Whether we have family or not, and even if we have not seen a nativity play for years, Jesus can be very real for all of us.

The story of nativity plays, whether recent memories or from long ago, can be with us all year round and the Christmas story shows us that Jesus is permanently here and God's love is for all.

As the angel said, "I bring you good news of great joy that will be for all the people." ▥

A Country Calendar For *Winter*

■ As January hits and winter reaches its fiercest, make sure your garden survives unscathed. Check stakes, fleeces, canes and all supports for damage – and don't forget to keep feeding the birds! Avoid cooking fat, margarines and oils in bird food – stick to fresh lard and beef suet.

■ Now's the time to start forcing rhubarb, if you're thinking of having a go. Rhubarb is a native plant of Siberia, so grows well in Britain in our cold, wet winters. In fact, the "Rhubarb Triangle" in West Yorkshire was once so productive that, at its peak, it produced 90% of the world's forced rhubarb and covered about 30 square miles!

"He who has not Christmas in his heart will never find it under a tree"

– Roy L. Smith.

■ One of nature's most portable fruits, clementines are a Christmas staple in Britain. Did you know that there are never less than seven and never more than 14 segments in each fruit?

Thinkstockphotos.